Carolina Friends School
Durham Early School

Water is Wet

by **Penny Pollock**

photographs by
Barbara Beirne

G.P. Putnam's Sons
New York

Acknowledgments

Many people helped make this book possible.

Parents gave generously of their time; children gave

their joyful spirits. We express our thanks to the families

involved, and to Lois Horn of the Village Nursery

School, who appreciates the child's view of life.

PP / BB

Text copyright © 1985 by Penny Pollock · Photographs copyright © 1985 by Barbara Beirne · All rights reserved. Published simultaneously in Canada by General Publishing Co. Limited, Toronto · Printed in the United States of America · Library of Congress Cataloging in Publication Data · Pollock, Penny. Water is wet.   Summary: Brief text and photographs introduce the characteristics and uses of water.   1. Water—Juvenile literature. [1. Water]   I. Beirne, Barbara, ill.   II. Title.   QD169.W3P65   1985   546'.22   84-11466   ISBN 0-399-21180-2   First impression

For Nora, who feels happy in the rain —PP

For Mother, who taught me to love the water —BB

You can do lots of things with water —

drink it,

play in it,

and let it dribble down your cheek.

You can pour water with a hose

or paint it
with a brush.

You can smack water with your boot,

whack it
with a stick,

or plunk it

with a rock.

Water is handy for washing your dog,

scrubbing
your pretend
baby's top

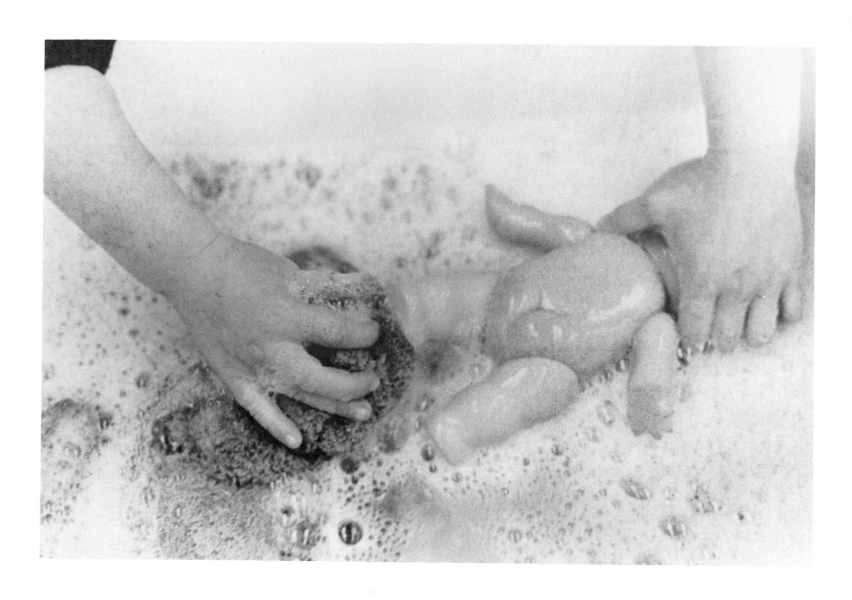

and bottom,

and bathing your real baby, too.

Water is fine

for helping things grow.

Water is great for making light bubbles

and heavy mud pies.

Rain is water from the sky. It "pings"

your umbrella and tickles your fingers.

When winter rain turns into snow,

skiing and sledding are the way to go.

Anyone you know?

When frozen water
turns to ice,
gliding on skates
can be nice.

Water is grand for jumping,

flopping,

and floating, too.

Water is wet —

and wonderful.

Carolina Friends School
Durham Early School